Y0-DWO-526

ALEXANDER *Hamilton*

SPIRIT
of America®

ALEXANDER *Hamilton*

By Pam Rosenberg

Content Adviser: Stephen Knott, Assistant Professor and Research Fellow, Miller Center of Public Affairs, University of Virginia, Charlottesville, Virginia

The Child's World®
Chanhassen, Minnesota

ALEXANDER *Hamilton*

Published in the United States of America by The Child's World®
P.O. Box 326 • Chanhassen, MN 55317-0326 • 800-599-READ • www.childsworld.com

Acknowledgments

The Child's World®: Mary Berendes, Publishing Director

Editorial Directions, Inc.: E. Russell Primm, Editorial Director and Line Editor; Katie Marsico, Assistant Editor; Matthew Messbarger, Editorial Assistant; Susan Hindman, Copy Editor; Susan Ashley, Proofreader; Julie Zaveloff, Chris Simms, and Peter Garnham, Fact Checkers; Tim Griffin/IndexServ, Indexer; Dawn Friedman, Photo Researcher; Linda S. Koutris, Photo Selector

The Design Lab: Kathleen Petelinsek, Art Direction; Kari Thornborough, Page Production

Photo

Cover: Archivo Iconografico, S.A./Corbis; Réunion des Musées Nationaux/Art Resource, NY: 9, 17; Archivo Iconografico, S.A./Corbis: 2; Tony Arruza/Corbis: 8; Layne Kennedy/Corbis: 11; Corbis: 13, 19; Profiles in History/Corbis: 18; Bettmann/Corbis: 20, 25, 27; Lee Snider/Corbis: 28; Roger Viollet/Getty Images: 16; The Granger Collection, New York: 10, 15, 22; North Wind Picture Archives: 6, 21.

Library of Congress Cataloging-in-Publication Data
Rosenberg, Pam.
  Alexander Hamilton : soldier and statesman / by Pam Rosenberg.
      v. cm.— (Our people)
Includes index.
Contents: A precocious boy—From student to soldier—Distinguished service—A life cut short.
  ISBN 1-59296-172-X (lib. bdg. : alk. paper)
  1. Hamilton, Alexander, 1757–1804—Juvenile literature. 2. Statesmen—United States—Biography—Juvenile literature. 3. United States—History—Revolution, 1775–1783—Juvenile literature.
4. United States—Politics and government—1783–1809—Juvenile literature. [1. Hamilton, Alexander, 1757–1804. 2. Statesmen.] I. Title. II. Series.
  E302.6.H2R68 2004
  973.4'092—dc22   2003018127

Contents

Chapter ONE   *An Intelligent Boy*   6

Chapter TWO   *From Student to Soldier*   12

Chapter THREE   *Distinguished Service*   18

Chapter FOUR   *A Life Cut Short*   26

Time Line   29

Glossary Terms   30

For Further Information   31

Index   32

ONE

An Intelligent Boy

Although Alexander Hamilton did not have an easy start in life, he grew up to become a distinguished politician. He is remembered today for the important role he played in developing the U.S. government and establishing a national economy.

TEN-YEAR-OLD ALEXANDER WAS HARD AT work. It was 1765, and the small, red-headed boy's father had recently left for Saint Kitts, a small island in the Caribbean. He had traveled to Saint Croix (another Caribbean island) on business, taking along his wife and sons. His wife, unwilling to tolerate the poor living conditions her husband was providing, remained in Saint Croix with her two sons. She set up her own business and was able to make a living for herself and the boys. While her older son, James, was not very good at the skills needed for running a business, young Alexander was a great help. He assisted her in running her small shop, doing the bookkeeping, and keeping track of the inventory.

When Alexander was about 13 years old, he went to work for Beekman and Cruger, an import-

6

export business based in New York. The firm did business in New York, England, and through-out the Caribbean islands. When his mother died in 1768, at least the boy had a job. Over the next few years, his boss, Nicholas Cruger, came to depend on him. The boy had an amazing talent for business.

Who was this young boy? You probably know him as Alexander Hamilton—one of the Founding Fathers of the United States of America.

Alexander Hamilton was born on January 11, 1755, on Nevis, an island in the Caribbean Sea. His mother, Rachel Fawcett, never formally married his father, James Hamilton. She had been married to a German Jewish man named Johann Michael Levine. She was only 16 and Levine was 38 when they married, and he treated his wife poorly. She left him and returned to live with her mother. She began living with James Hamilton when she was 21 and gave birth to their first son, James, in 1753.

The older Hamilton was the fourth son of a wealthy Scottish lord. As the fourth son, he knew there was no chance of an inheritance, so he settled in Nevis to try to support himself as a merchant. Unfortunately, Hamilton was lazy and not a very good businessman. He and Rachel and their sons lived in poverty.

Rachel Hamilton believed in education. She made sure Alexander attended school. Rachel came

Alexander Hamilton's father grew up in a castle in Scotland. Shenistone Castle was purchased by James Hamilton's great-grandfather in 1685 and renamed The Grange. When Alexander Hamilton's home in New York was completed in 1802, he named it The Grange, after his ancestors' home in Scotland.

from a French family, and Alexander learned to speak French at home from his mother and grandmother. So, it wasn't surprising that after his mother's death, he longed to continue his education and make something of himself.

Unfortunately, that didn't seem possible. In the 1700s, a person's social position in life was very

This museum in Nevis is built on the foundation of the home in which Hamilton was born. The original house was 160 years old when it was destroyed by an earthquake in 1840.

Ships loaded with sugar for export prepare to leave a Caribbean port. The sugar trade played a major role in the economy of Saint Croix during the 1700s.

important. As the son of unwed parents with little money, he found it hard to imagine how he could rise above his position as a clerk for Beekman and Cruger. Then, in October 1771, Nicholas Cruger became ill. He left Saint Croix and returned to New York, leaving the management of his business to young Hamilton. With business skills and a level of maturity rarely found in such a young man, Hamilton quickly made a name for himself among the merchants and ships' captains on the island. When Cruger returned early in March 1772, he was pleased with how well the 17-year-old Hamilton had managed his business.

Interesting Fact

Some historians believe that Hamilton was born in 1757. This is the year Hamilton himself said that he was born. When his mother's estate was being settled after her death, the court records stated that Hamilton was 13 years old, which would make the 1755 date correct. Some people believe that Hamilton used the 1757 date to make himself seem like more of a genius.

When Alexander Hamilton was growing up in the Caribbean, he saw the effects of slavery firsthand. As a result, he was a lifelong opponent of slavery.

Just as coffee, cotton, and sugar were exported from the Caribbean to Europe, enslaved Africans were regularly imported to plantations on islands such as Saint Croix. Unlike many other famous politicians of his time, Hamilton refused to own slaves.

Another man impressed by Hamilton was the Reverend Hugh Knox. He was the minister of the Presbyterian church where Hamilton attended services. Knox could see how intelligent Hamilton was and invited him to make use of the many books he kept in his personal library. After a time, the minister realized that the boy would need to leave Saint Croix to further his education. He arranged for a scholarship for Hamilton to continue his education in New York, getting contributions from the businessmen who had been impressed with Hamilton's work. In early October 1772, Hamilton set sail for America. He would never set foot in the Caribbean again.

Nevis is an island in the eastern Caribbean Sea. It is shaped like a circle and surrounded by coral reefs. Most of the island is a mountain called Nevis Peak. The entire area of Nevis is about 36 square miles (93 square kilometers). Its climate is mild. The average temperature is about 80° Fahrenheit (27° Celsius) and the island gets about 55 inches (140 centimeters) of rain each year.

The island was spotted by Christopher Columbus in 1493. The name of the island comes from Columbus's description of the clouds above Nevis Peak. He called them *las nieves*—"the snows" in Spanish. During Alexander Hamilton's life, the island was a British colony. Many white settlers made their living there as sugarcane plantation owners or managers, or as merchants involved in the sugar trade. Today, the island is an independent member of the British Commonwealth known as the Federation of Saint Kitts and Nevis.

TWO

From Student to Soldier

ALEXANDER HAMILTON ARRIVED IN BOSTON IN October 1772. After exploring the city for a week, he took the stagecoach to his destination—New York City. His plan was to study medicine at the College of New Jersey, now known as Princeton University. When he arrived, he was introduced to Hercules Mulligan, who was to be Hamilton's guardian. He and Hamilton quickly became friends, and Mulligan treated Hamilton like a son.

The friendship between the two men influenced the direction Hamilton's life took. Mulligan was a member of the Sons of Liberty, a radical group that had formed in 1765 to oppose the Stamp Act. Members of the group continued to speak out against control of the American colonies by the British king. He introduced the young Hamilton to William Livingston and Elias Boudinot, who both took Hamilton under their wing. A few years later, Livingston and Boudinot would lead

New Jersey during the American Revolution. Both helped pay for Hamilton's education and remained Hamilton's political supporters for the rest of his life.

Hamilton's early education had not prepared him for college. He spent a year studying at Elizabethtown Academy in Elizabethtown, New Jersey. When he applied for admission to the College of New Jersey, he requested that he be allowed to study at his own pace, to complete his education more quickly. His request was turned down. He then applied to King's College—now known as Columbia University—in New York. The president of King's College agreed to his request. In the autumn of 1773, Hamilton returned to New York and began his college education. King's College was known at the time for being a "Tory" college. Its president, Dr. Myles Cooper, was a British **Loyalist** who taught his political views to his students. Hamilton had a

William Livingston was elected the first governor of New Jersey in 1776. He served so well that he was reelected until his death in 1790.

great deal of respect for Cooper, even though the two men held different political views.

On December 16, 1773, about three months after Hamilton began his studies at King's College, the Boston Tea Party took place. News of this event reached the Sons of Liberty in New York. In spring of the following year, they staged their own "tea party" and Hamilton was there. He later said that he wasn't, because he was afraid he would be expelled from King's College if it became known that he was associated with the Sons of Liberty. Soon after that tea party, however, Hamilton began writing anonymous newspaper articles in support of the **Patriots.**

In September 1774, the First Continental Congress met in Philadelphia, Pennsylvania. The American colonies were edging closer and closer to war with Great Britain. When he first arrived in New York in 1773, Hamilton had said that he supported loyalty to England. But over time and with much study of the issues, he became an outspoken supporter of revolution. When an Anglican priest who identified himself only as "A Farmer" published a pamphlet that spoke out against the Continental Congress, Hamilton was inspired to write a pamphlet in response. *A Full Vindication of the Measures of Congress* was published in December 1774. When "A Farmer"—Dr. Samuel Seabury—responded,

Hamilton replied with a new pamphlet, *The Farmer Refuted.*

Then, on April 19, 1775, the war of words became a war of bullets. The first battle of the American Revolution was fought in Lexington, Massachusetts. Hamilton immediately enlisted in the New York **militia.** His company drilled every

Hamilton addresses a crowd from the steps at King's College. He was an excellent student but is probably better known for the fiery speeches he made on issues surrounding American independence.

morning, wearing leather caps with the words "Freedom or Death" printed on them. Hamilton had once written a letter to a friend saying that he wished there would be a war. Because he didn't come from a rich or upper-class family, he felt that one of the best ways he could make a name for himself would be to fight bravely in a war. He now had the opportunity he had hoped for.

Young Hamilton was a courageous soldier whose military talents eventually gained the attention of higher-ranking officers. Early on, he was noted for his service in the battles of White Plains and Long Island, which took place in New York, and also in the battles of Trenton and Princeton, which occurred in New Jersey.

HERCULES MULLIGAN WAS BORN IN COUNTY ANTRIM, IRELAND. WHEN HE came to America, he settled in New York City and opened a men's clothing store. He provided custom-tailored clothing to some of the wealthiest residents of New York. In 1776, the British captured Mulligan. After a short time as a prisoner of war, the British released Mulligan. It was often the custom at the time to release prisoners who were considered to be gentlemen. Mulligan was **paroled** on the condition that he would not leave New York City.

Shortly after his parole, Mulligan risked being recaptured and met up with Hamilton. The two men apparently agreed to a plan. Mulligan would return to New York City and act as a spy for General George Washington (right), the Continental army's commander-in-chief. Mulligan made clothing for many British and Loyalist officers at his store. While these men were having clothing made, they talked about their war plans. Mulligan was able to provide Washington with information that often helped the Continental army plan its war strategy.

Chapter THREE

Distinguished Service

A letter written by Hamilton during his service as an aide-de-camp to George Washington. Between 1777 and 1781, Hamilton didn't spend much time in battle. His work as an aide-de-camp helped him polish the political and problem-solving skills that would be put to good use later in his career.

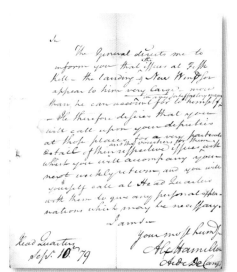

HAMILTON BECAME A CAPTAIN IN THE NEW YORK army. He organized his own artillery company and exhibited great leadership and bravery as he commanded his men. His skills did not go unnoticed. George Washington, then commander in chief of the Continental army, asked Hamilton to become an aide-de-camp in January 1777. This was an important position at army headquarters.

General Washington's aides wrote out orders and composed letters for him. Often, they delivered the messages as well. This correspondence was the only way Washington could communicate with his officers, spies, suppliers, the Continental Congress, and others working for the revolutionary cause. There were no telegraphs, radios, or other means of communication at the time.

Hamilton accepted the position as aide-de-camp. He soon became an important

member of Washington's staff. When the French agreed to help the American cause, Hamilton's fluent French made him even more valuable to Washington. He was able to serve as an interpreter and compose letters to French officers in their own language.

Unfortunately for Hamilton, however, Washington became so dependent on his brilliant young aide that he was unwilling to let him serve in any other way. Over the course of the war, Hamilton requested several times that he be given the command of troops. Washington always turned him down. This was frustrating for Hamilton, who longed to distinguish himself in battle. Finally, in 1781, Hamilton was growing increasingly tired of the paperwork and his duties as Washington's assistant. He argued with Washington and quit his job.

Interesting Fact

Hamilton had married Elizabeth Schuyler on December 14, 1780. The daughter of General Philip Schuyler, she was a member of one of New York's wealthiest and most influential families. After resigning his position as Washington's aide, Hamilton returned to his wife at the Schuyler mansion and spent his time studying in his father-in-law's well-stocked library. During this time, he began to come up with some of the ideas about America's financial problems that would serve him well in the years to come.

In the summer of 1781, Hamilton once again asked Washington to give him the command of troops. This time, Washington agreed and put him in charge of a battalion in New York. Hamilton led his men bravely during the decisive Battle of Yorktown. Britain's General Cornwallis and his troops surrendered on October 19, 1781, and the war began to come to an end. The Treaty of Paris, signed on September 3, 1783, officially ended the war.

After his service in the war, Hamilton studied law and was admitted to practice in 1782. His son Philip was born on January 22, 1782. He and his wife went on to have seven more children. Hamilton was elected to the Continental Congress as a representative of New York. He served from November 1782 to July 1783. It was during this time that he became more and more convinced that the new United States of America needed a strong central government.

From 1783 to 1787, Hamilton practiced law in New York City and served in the New York state legislature. He played an important part in calling for the Constitutional Convention that met in Philadelphia in May 1787. The participants planned to revise the Articles of Confederation (the first set of laws governing the United States), but instead ended up writing a new **constitution.** Hamilton strongly supported this new constitution, which provided for a strong national—or federal—government.

When he returned to New York, he worked hard to increase support for the new constitution. He began writing *The Federalist* under the **pseudonym**

Cornwallis surrenders to Washington at the Battle of Yorktown. In addition to unofficially ending the American Revolution, the surrender resulted in 8,000 British soldiers becoming prisoners of war.

of Publius and with the assistance of James Madison and John Jay. This series of articles was published in newspapers between October 1787 and May 1788. *The Federalist* helped explain how the new federal government would work and convinced many people to support the new constitution. Though there were many people opposed to the constitution, Hamilton's arguments helped to convince New York's leaders to approve it.

When George Washington was elected president in 1789, he appointed Alexander Hamilton as the first U.S. secretary of the treasury. Hamilton's main goals as a cabinet member were to establish credit for the new United States and strengthen the national government. He began an intensive study of the country's finances in order to create a plan that would

Pages from The Federalist. *Alexander Hamilton wrote these articles under the pseudonym Publius because it was the name of an important and well-respected politician in ancient Rome.*

reduce the huge debt the United States had piled up during the war. His early business and financial training helped him in this new position.

In 1790–1791, he wrote four reports that laid out what he believed needed to be done to ensure that the United States could compete financially with other countries. The first two reports were jointly titled *Reports on the Public Credit.* They called for the federal government to take over the states' war debts and for Congress to create a system of taxes that would be used to pay those debts. Many congressmen were opposed to Hamilton's plan.

To get Congress to go along with his plan, he had to make a deal with Thomas Jefferson. This was not something that Hamilton would do easily. He and Thomas Jefferson were political enemies. The two men had different opinions on many matters that affected the country. For example, Hamilton believed in a strong national government, while Jefferson believed that the states should keep more power for themselves. The disagreements between the two men led to the formation of two political parties—the Federalists led by Hamilton and the Democratic-Republicans led by Jefferson. This was the beginning of the two-party political system that is still in use in the United States today.

With Jefferson in a position of importance—not only with his political party but also as Washington's secretary of state—Hamilton put aside his differences with him and made a deal. Jefferson got southern congressmen to agree to the financial plan. In return, Hamilton had to support locating the U.S. capital on the Potomac River.

The third report that Hamilton wrote— *Report on a National Bank*—called for the creation of the Bank of the United States. Congress approved the charter for the bank and Washington signed it. It is through Hamilton's efforts that the young country was able to manage the debt left over from the revolution and create a national currency (or money) that could be used by all U.S. citizens.

The fourth report that Hamilton wrote was the *Report on Manufactures.* This report showed that Hamilton understood better than other men of his time that the Industrial Revolution would eventually cross the Atlantic and make its way to the United States. He called for various laws to protect new U.S. industries. He believed that the federal government needed to look out for its manufacturers because they would become the most important part of the economy. Because most people in the United States made their living from farming or businesses related to farming, Congress never did anything with the report. But reading it now shows how well Hamilton understood the forces that were beginning to shape the world's economy.

ELIZABETH SCHUYLER HAMILTON WAS BORN ON AUGUST 9, 1757. HER FAMILY and close friends called her Betsy or Eliza for short. Though she was not one of the great beauties of her time, she was an attractive woman. Alexander Hamilton once described her as "most unmercifully handsome."

Betsy Schuyler grew up in a mansion in Albany, New York. Her father was the descendant of one of the first settlers of the colony that became the state of New York. She grew up surrounded by rich and powerful people.

Betsy was a strong young woman who enjoyed the outdoors. She spoke English, Dutch, and French and was an excellent artist. Hamilton began courting her during the winter of 1780 in Morristown, New Jersey.

Though Hamilton was unfaithful to his wife during their marriage, she remained faithful to him, even after his death. Only 47 years old when Hamilton died, she spent the next 50 years editing his papers and making sure that he was remembered for his great accomplishments. She died in 1854 at the age of 97.

FOUR

A Life Cut Short

Interesting Fact

▶ The members of the House of Representatives voted 36 times before the tie between Jefferson and Burr was broken and Jefferson was elected president of the United States.

ALEXANDER HAMILTON WAS A MAN WITH VERY definite opinions. Other leaders of the U.S. government didn't always agree with him. Over time, he made some bitter political enemies. One of these men was Aaron Burr.

In 1791, after organizing a group of politicians against Hamilton's father-in-law, Burr won election to the U.S. Senate. Hamilton was not happy with this turn of events. Then, in the election of 1800, Burr was nominated as the vice presidential candidate of the Republican Party led by Thomas Jefferson. The party's presidential candidate was Jefferson. Under the electoral system at the time, however, electors didn't vote for a presidential candidate and a vice presidential candidate. Instead, the person with the highest number of votes became president and the person with the second-highest number of votes became vice president. Burr and Jefferson won the same number of electoral votes. The members of the House of

Aaron Burr (second from left) and Alexander Hamilton (far right) preparing to duel. Before the American Revolution, dueling was considered an acceptable—though dangerous—way to settle differences. By 1804, however, it was illegal in several states. After killing Hamilton, Burr was charged with murder and was forced to give up his political career.

Representatives had to vote to break the tie. Although Burr had agreed to run as a vice presidential candidate, he now saw the opportunity to become president. But Hamilton took this opportunity to stir up opposition to Burr's candidacy, and he lost his bid for the presidency.

Hamilton and Burr remained bitter political enemies. In 1804, Burr was nominated for governor of New York. Hamilton vigorously opposed Burr's election, and he was defeated. Weeks later, Burr accused Hamilton of **slandering** him. Burr demanded that Hamilton write him an apology. When Hamilton refused, Burr challenged him to a **duel.** On July 11, 1804, Hamilton faced Burr in a duel at Weehawken, New Jersey. According to his **second,** Hamilton planned to fire into the air. He believed this would allow both men to keep their

Interesting Fact

The inscription on Hamilton's tombstone reads: "The patriot of incorruptible integrity, the soldier of approved valour, the statesman of consummate wisdom, where talents and virtue will be admired by grateful posterity long after this marble shall have moldered into dust."

honor while avoiding injury. Burr, however, had no such plan. Burr fired a split second before Hamilton. His shot pierced Hamilton's liver. Hamilton's shot hit a tree branch overhead.

Alexander Hamilton died 31 hours later at the age of 49. It was a senseless end to a brilliant life. Playing many roles—aide to General Washington during the Revolution, author of *The Federalist,* first secretary of the treasury—Hamilton helped create the United States of America we know today.

This statue in New York City's Central Park honors the life and accomplishments of Alexander Hamilton.

1755 Alexander Hamilton is born on January 11 on the island of Nevis.

1765 The Sons of Liberty organize in England's American colonies; Hamilton's father returns to Saint Kitts, leaving his family behind on Saint Croix.

1771 Hamilton's boss, Nicholas Cruger, leaves him in charge of his business while he travels to New York.

1772 Hamilton sails to Boston and then travels on to New York to continue his education.

1773 Hamilton begins his studies at King's College in New York City; the Boston Tea Party takes place on December 16.

1774 The First Continental Congress meets in Philadelphia, Pennsylvania; Hamilton publishes *A Full Vindication of the Measures of Congress*.

1777 George Washington asks Hamilton to join his staff at the Continental army's headquarters.

1780 Hamilton marries Elizabeth Schuyler on December 14.

1781 Hamilton resigns as aide-de-camp to General Washington; Hamilton commands a New York battalion in the decisive Battle of Yorktown; Britain's General Cornwallis surrenders on October 19.

1782 Hamilton is admitted to the practice of law; he serves as New York representative to the Continental Congress from November 1782 to July 1783.

1783 Hamilton begins practicing law in New York City and serving as a member of the New York state legislature.

1787 Hamilton participates in the Constitutional Convention and strongly supports the newly written constitution; the first of the essays that would become *The Federalist* is published.

1789 George Washington is elected president of the United States and appoints Hamilton as the first secretary of the treasury.

1790 Hamilton begins writing a series of reports that outline his financial plan for the country.

1804 Burr runs for governor of New York and Hamilton campaigns against him; Burr shoots Hamilton in a duel, and Hamilton dies on July 12.

constitution (kon-stuh-TOO-shuhn)
A constitution is a written set of laws that lists the rights of the people and powers of the government of a country. The Constitution of the United States was written at the Constitutional Convention of 1787.

duel (DOO-uhl)
A duel is a fight between two people using swords or guns as weapons. Aaron Burr challenged Alexander Hamilton to a duel.

Loyalist (LOI-uhl-ist)
A loyalist was a colonist who remained loyal to Great Britain during the American Revolution. Dr. Myles Cooper, the president of King's College, was a Loyalist.

militia (muh-LISH-uh)
A militia is a group of citizens who are trained to fight in the event of an emergency. Alexander Hamilton enlisted in the New York militia when the American Revolution began.

paroled (puh-ROLD)
A prisoner who is paroled is released early on the condition that he or she will obey the law. Hercules Mulligan was paroled on the condition that he would not leave New York City.

Patriots (PAY-tree-uhts)
The colonists who opposed the British and wanted to gain independence for the American colonies were known as the Patriots. Alexander Hamilton wrote anonymous newspaper articles in support of the Patriots.

pseudonym (SOOD-uh-nim)
A pseudonym is a false name—often called a pen name—used by an author instead of his real name. Hamilton used the pseudonym Publius when writing *The Federalist.*

second (SEK-uhnd)
In a duel, a second is a person's alternate. It is the duty of the seconds to try to reconcile the two parties without resorting to violence. According to his second, Hamilton planned to fire into the air instead of at Burr.

slandering (SLAN-dur-ing)
Slandering is the act of saying something that isn't true about someone and, by doing so, damaging the person's reputation. Aaron Burr accused Alexander Hamilton of slandering him.

INFORMATION

Web Sites

Visit our home page for lots of links about Alexander Hamilton:
http://www.childsworld.com/links.html

Note to Parents, Teachers, and Librarians:
We routinely verify our Web links to make sure they're safe,
active sites—so encourage your readers to check them out!

Books

Collier, James Lincoln. *The Alexander Hamilton You Never Knew.* Danbury,
Conn.: Children's Press, 2003.

DeCarolis, Lisa. *Alexander Hamilton: Federalist and Founding Father.* New York:
PowerKids Press, 2003.

Jones, Veda Boyd. *Alexander Hamilton: First U.S. Secretary of the Treasury.*
Philadelphia: Chelsea House, 2000.

Places to Visit or Contact

Nevis Historical and Conservation Society
To learn more about Hamilton and his birthplace in the Caribbean
P.O. Box 563
Charlestown, Nevis, West Indies
869/469-5786

Hamilton Grange National Memorial
To visit Hamilton's home in upper Manhattan, New York
287 Convent Avenue
New York, NY 10005
212/283-5154

American Revolution, 13, 15, 20, *21*
Articles of Confederation, 21

Bank of the United States, 24
Battle of Yorktown, 20, *21*
Boston Tea Party, 14
Boudinot, Elias, 12–13
Burr, Aaron, 26–27, *27*

Caribbean, 6, 7, *8, 9,* 11, *11*
College of New Jersey, 12, 13
Columbia University, 14
Columbus, Christopher, 11
Continental army, 17
Continental Congress, 14, 18, 21
Cooper, Myles, 13–14
Cruger, Nicholas, 7, 9–10

Democratic-Republican Party, 23, 26
dueling, 27–28, *27*

Elizabethtown Academy, 13

The Farmer Refuted pamphlet, 15
The Federalist articles, 21–22, *22*
Federalist Party, 23
Federation of Saint Kitts and Nevis, 11
First Continental Congress, 14
A Full Vindication of the Measures of Congress pamphlet, 14

George II, king of England, 14
The Grange home, 8

Hamilton, Alexander, *6, 15, 27, 28*
as aide-de-camp, 18, *18,* 19
birth, 7, 9
childhood, 7
death, 25, 27, 28
education, 8, 10, 12, 13
law career, 20, 21
marriage, 20
military career, 15–16, *16,* 18, 19, 20
nickname, 20
as treasury secretary, 22–23

writings, 14, 15, 21–22, 22, 23, 24
Hamilton, Angelica (daughter), 28
Hamilton, Elizabeth Schuyler (wife), 20, 25, *25*
Hamilton, James (father), 6, 7, 8
Hamilton, James, Jr. (brother), 6–7
Hamilton, Philip (son), 21, 28
Hamilton, Rachel Fawcett (mother), 6, 7, 8

Industrial Revolution, 24

Jay, John, 22
Jefferson, Thomas, 23–24, 26–27

King's College, 13, 14, *15*
Knox, Henry, 23
Knox, Hugh, 10

Lafayette, Marquis de, *19*
Levine, Johann Michael, 7
Livingston, William, 12–13, *13*

Loyalists, 13

Madison, James, 22
Mulligan, Hercules, 12, 17

Nevis Island, 7, 8, 11, *11*

Patriots, 14

Randolph, Edmund, 23
Report on a National Bank, 24
Report on Manufactures, 24
Reports on the Public Credit, 23

Schuyler, Philip, 20, *20*
Seabury, Samuel, 14–15
Shenistone Castle, 8
slavery, 10, *10*
Sons of Liberty, 12, 14
Stamp Act, 12

Treaty of Paris, 20

Washington, George, 17, *17,* 18, 19–20, *19, 21,* 22, 24

About the Author

PAM ROSENBERG IS A FORMER JUNIOR HIGH SCHOOL TEACHER and corporate trainer. She currently works as an author and editor of children's books. She has always loved reading and feels very fortunate to be doing work that requires her to read all the time. When she isn't writing or editing books, she enjoys spending time with her husband and their two children, and reading just for fun. She lives in Chicago, Illinois.

32